IMAGES OF ENGLAND

# TILLINGBOURNE VALLEY

IMAGES OF ENGLAND

# TILLINGBOURNE VALLEY

MICHAEL MILLER

The History Press

First published 1996 by The Chalford Publishing Company

Reprinted 2017 by
The History Press
The Mill, Brimscombe Port
Stroud, Gloucestershire, GL5 2QG
www.thehistorypress.co.uk

Copyright © Michael Miller, 1996

ISBN 978 0 7524 0370 0

Typesetting and origination by The Chalford Publishing Company
Printed in Great Britain by TJ International Ltd, Padstow, Cornwall

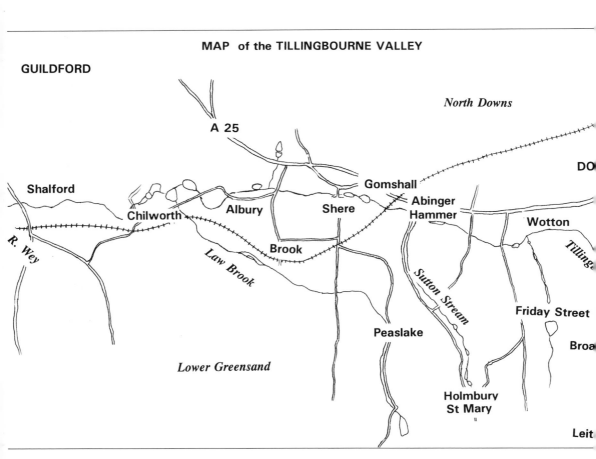

MAP of the TILLINGBOURNE VALLEY

GUILDFORD

North Downs

A 25

DO

Shalford

Gomshall

Abinger
Hammer

Wotton

Chilworth

Albury

Shere

Brook

Law Brook

R. Wey

Tilling

Sutton Stream

Friday Street

Broa

Peaslake

Lower Greensand

Holmbury
St Mary

Leit

# Contents

Acknowledgements                                        6

Introduction                                            7

1.    Source                                            9

2.    Switzerland in Surrey                            19

3.    The Glade in the Hills                           31

4.    The Hammer in the Valley                         39

5.    A Tannery in the Garden                          51

6.    The Prettiest in England                         67

7.    The Village that Moved                           83

8.    The Rill from the Hill                          101

9.    Damnable Inventions                             107

10.   A Shallow Ford                                  119

Bibliography                                          128

# Acknowledgements

I would like to thank the following who have given most generously of their time and information and granted permission for me to use their material:

Nigel Balchin, Albert Carter, Malcolm Covey, Terry Disley,
Margaret Evershed, Keith Harding, Sally Schupke, June Tiller, Elizabeth Rich,
Matthew Alexander and Guildford Museum,
John Janaway of the Surrey Local Studies Library, Dorking Museum,
Dorking Library and the Lambeth Archives at the Minet Library.

There must also be others with whom I have spoken over the years but cannot now identify. If I have quoted or misquoted anyone without due acknowledgement, I apologise most sincerely.

# Introduction

The area of Surrey known as the Tillingbourne Valley lies between Guildford and Dorking and the picturesque villages along the river and the surrounding countryside have long since attracted both visitors and settlers alike. The Greensand Hills rise to their highest point at Leith Hill in Surrey and their geological strata promote the collection and filtration of rainwater which on encountering the gault clay is discharged through springs. It is one such egress on the gentle northern slopes which is the origin of our bourne.

Stoneage man would have been attracted by the availability of a continuous supply of water to slake his thirst, cook his food, and clean his hides. This area was settled long before the wild wealden forests to the south. Only the occasional foray was necessary to provide additional grazing for animals and timber for fuel and building. Evidence of these missions can be seen today in the preponderance of north – south roads and the deep cuts in the sandstone hills produced over millennia by a combination of human and animal feet. The Pilgrims Way, running from east to west, also has its origins long before Chaucer and his tales of pilgrimage to Canterbury.

Having begun its journey northwards, the river swings to the west on reaching the chalk downs and meanders across the meadows in the valley bottom between the sandstone hills to the south and the chalk ridge to the north. Tributaries from Friday Street, Holmbury and Peaslake contribute to the Tillingbourne until it finally joins the Wey at Shalford Meadows.

Thus it would have continued had not the hand of man intervened. The Domesday Book records several mills in the area and by the middle ages the water power of the Tillingbourne worked water wheels for the grinding of corn, and the fulling of cloth prior to dyeing. Human manipulation of water power was developed throughout the sixteenth and seventeenth century for the working of a great variety of industrial contrivances. Foremost in the art were the Evelyns of Wotton who were involved initially in the manufacture of gunpowder but diversified into drawing brass wire and smelting iron. Remoteness and the abundance of timber were decisive for its location but, when the gunpowder works at Wotton were destroyed by an explosion, it was considered prudent to move the operation further down stream to Chilworth. Although the Evelyns were the most ambitious of the industrial developers or 'projectors' as they were known, the Hills of Abinger, the Randalls of Chilworth, and the Brays of Shere also undertook industrial ventures.

Grinding of gunpowder and wood pulp for making paper, especially bank notes became particular specialities of the area. William Cobbett visited the valley on one of his 'rural rides' and nothing delighted him more in Surrey than 'the narrow and exquisitely beautiful vale of Chilworth'. However, he subsequently accused the mill owners of 'carrying into execution two of the most damnable inventions that ever sprang from the minds of man under the influence of the devil, namely the making of gunpowder and of bank-notes!' On further reflection he conceded the value of paper in providing a register for recording his observations. Gunpowder from the valley has played a significant role in battles from the Civil War to the First World War.

Much of the design and construction of Albury Park gardens is also attributed to John Evelyn at the behest of his friend and neighbour Henry Howard, later sixth Duke of Norfolk. Although legend surrounds the origins of the Silent Pool, in reality it was dug to provide a source of water for Howard's ambitious water gardens scheme which included a half moon pond and fountain as well as an eighty-foot wide canal. The mill pond at Friday Street also owes its origins to the Evelyn family and although the mill has not been in use since 1736 the old mill house and the fishponds can still be seen from the footpath below the dam wall.

As steam, and later electricity, replaced water as the primary source of industrial power, so the mills along the Tillingbourne gradually closed, some being adapted to other purposes. Notable amongst these was the use of the old mill ponds for the cultivation of watercress, for which the firm of Coes of Abinger became nationally renowned. The arrival of the railway in the nineteenth century encouraged further diversification of the area's various industries, and tempted many of London's workers to settle there permanently. Whilst the occasional motorist or rambler will be immediately struck by its natural beauty, few will be aware of the past events which have contrived to change its shape and challenge its tranquillity. Most of the images in this compilation recall a way of life now sadly lost except in the memories of the older generation.

Michael Miller
Cranleigh 1996

# One

# Source

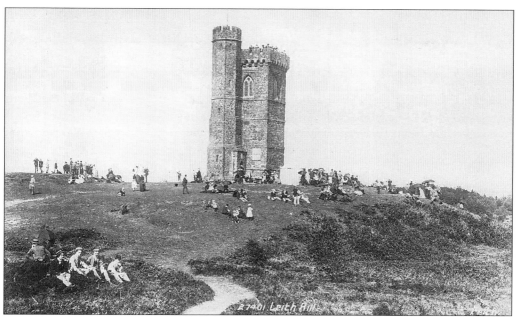

Leith Hill rises to 965 feet and is the highest point in Surrey. The geological structure comprised of greensand and gault clay gives rise to aquifers which emerge from the slopes in the form of a virtually constant flow of clear pure water. The source of the Tillingbourne is from one such egress close to the area known as Tilling Springs.

The path from Leith Hill joins Sheephouse Lane and passes through the hamlet of Broadmoor whose origins are related to the nearby Brookmill. The surrounding woods provided fuel for gunpowder making and evidence given in 1609 refers to 'six new cottages and a mill erected on the common of the Manwood'.

This row of detached cottages was built around a central reading room in the 1880s as a philanthropic gesture by Arthur Brooke. Many walkers pass this way, finding it a tranquil resting place between Leith Hill and Dorking.

The Old Cottage remains largely unchanged from when this picture was taken in 1902. The sheep have been replaced by motor cars and the undergrowth has been allowed to encroach. Until around 1960 the residents of Broadmoor took their water from the stream and, when water was at last laid on, at least one of the old residents refused to use it, preferring to continue with a bucket from the spring.

Pinehurst is a collection of cottages in the valley below Broadmoor. The sender of this postcard has marked the place where he stayed in 1927, describing it as 'a 200-year old cottage, tiny bedrooms, enormous fire – half a tree'. The larger building on the left is now a riding school.

The Rest-a-Wyle is an appropriately named hostelry in Broadmoor run as a tea-room by Mrs W. Lacey in the 1930s. No doubt it offered a welcome rest with tea and cakes to countless ramblers but it seems to have disappeared around the time of the Second World War.

The ornamental cascade near Broadmoor was constructed in the eighteenth century as part of a garden landscape for the cottage to the north, known as Lonesome Lodge. Judging from earlier descriptions, it formed part of an elaborate scheme and is served by a leat higher up the valley. Today it can be seen in its former glory again due to the recent work of volunteers.

Between Broadmoor and Wotton the stream passes through a series of chain ponds thought to be the work of members of the Evelyn family of Wotton. In his diary for 1643, John Evelyn wrote, 'I built by my brother's permission a study, made a fishpond, an island and some other solitudes at Wotton'.

John Evelyn learnt many of the skills of the water engineer following a trip to Italy. The fountain shown is no longer functional but is reminiscent of similar features at Chatsworth and Castle Howard.

Tillingbourne House seems to have begun life as a steward's lodge, built for the Duke of Norfolk around 1840, entirely from local stone. The Duke often stayed here when travelling between Arundel and London. Later the house was enlarged and considerable improvements made to the grounds.

In 1904 the house was occupied by a Mr Ricardo but it became vacant in the thirties. It was taken over by the army in 1941 but after the war was found to be severely affected by dry rot and was demolished in the 1960s. Several new houses have been built in the grounds which benefit from the original water features.

Workers' cottages at Dearleap, Wotton, in 1900. This remote and somewhat isolated community would have been home for many of the artisans and tradesmen employed by the Evelyn family to work on the Wotton Estate.

The Wotton Hatch has provided hospitality to passing travellers since the eighteenth century and at one time provided stabling for eight horses. The name 'hatch' is an old Saxon word meaning 'gate' but its significance is barely perceptible today.

Wotton fire brigade was funded by the Evelyn family and crewed by villagers and estate workers, and is seen here setting off from the Wotton Hatch. The hand pump dates from 1875 and was acquired by the Evelyn family shortly afterwards. It lay forgotten until 1967 when it was found in a barn and restored by men at the Dorking fire station and can be seen at the Fire Service Museum in Reigate.

The village band pose outside the Wotton Hatch in 1906. The band was supported by the Evelyn family and played at village events.

# Two
# Switzerland in Surrey

FRIDAY STREET, ABINGER.

The area known as Friday Street has long been a favourite venue for day trippers, despite its remoteness. The lake lies on a tributary of the Tillingbourne and was created when the stream was dammed in the late sixteenth century.

Abinger Bottom is a tiny hamlet with traces of a mill pond to the south. A spring rises near here and flows down towards Friday Street. The well-worn path over the hill leads to Abinger Common, the nearest source of essential supplies for the villagers before the use of wheeled vehicles.

Whilst most supplies would have to be brought in, there was at one time a bakery in the cottage on the right. Later a muffin man came from Guildford by train to Gomshall and walked as far as Abinger Bottom with a tray on his head, ringing a bell to attract customers.

The path from Abinger Bottom follows the line of the rill, passes through a group of old cottages and on to the welcome hostelry of the Stephan Langton. The building to the side of the Stephan Langton was once the local bakery owned by the Dixon family. An old railway carriage was provided with a temporary roof and pressed into service as tea rooms, where guests were able to enjoy freshly baked bread and cakes.

The Stephan Langton has long been a popular place for ramblers and visitors to Friday Street to take refreshment. The street is named after the well known Archbishop of Canterbury who was said to have been born there but this assertion almost certainly derives from a work of fiction by local author, Martin Tupper.

The lake and its surroundings enjoyed a new-found popularity with the invention of the motor car. These day trippers partake of the pleasurable pastime of paddling in the shallow waters of the lake.

The damming of the stream and creation of the lake occurred in the late sixteenth century. Although in use in 1604 the corn mill may have found even earlier application as a gunpowder mill. The mills were closed in 1736, most probably for aesthetic reasons, and the tenant moved to Abinger.

The mill house at Friday Street still stands below the dam. A deed of 1616 describes the site as a 'watermill millhouse, wheels, millstones, lately erected on Wotton common, together with floodgates, sluices and mill ponds'.

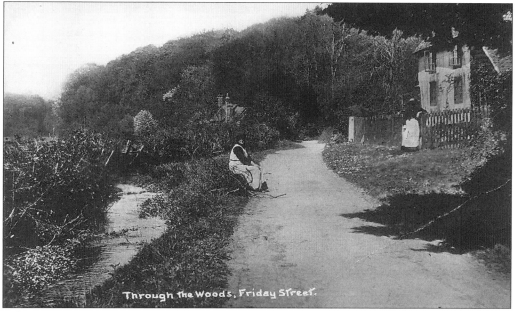

Below the mill house the path continues on through the woods towards Wotton. A series of fish ponds were created by various members of the Evelyn family and the closing of the mill was probably to ensure sufficient flow of water. The path crosses the stream at a point known locally as Pug's Corner.

When the cottagers grazed their cattle on Abinger Common the free grazing was contained by gates across the public roads, traces of which can still be seen. The cottage on the left was for many years a shop and post office run by William Mott and later his wife Charlotte. The pond opposite became known as Mott's pond and was later filled in.

Goddards was built in 1899 from a design of Sir Edwyn Lutyens with a garden laid out by Gertrude Jekyll. The design provides for two wings joined by a central common room over which was a games room. After this picture was taken Lutyens was called back to add two further wings and today the house remains virtually to this design.

In 1893 when the glebe land at Abinger Common was being developed a water diviner was called in by Mr W. J. Evelyn and water was located at an estimated depth of 150 feet. A well was sunk by Messrs King of Abinger Hammer and water was struck at 152 feet. The well was dedicated to St James and a plaque reminds us that it was given for the use of parishioners.

The Abinger Hatch has been providing hospitality for working men and 'excursionists' for over a century. With six bedrooms and three reception rooms it was well able to cater for the motor trade, charabanc parties, hikers and ramblers. Among others, the comediennes Elsie and Doris Walters were regular visitors.

When the manor of Wotton was conveyed to the Evelyn family in 1579 there began a series of improvements, additions and enlargements unparalleled in any other property in the region. The fountain was constructed by the diarist John Evelyn around 1652 following a Grand Tour of Europe in which he was impressed by the skills of the Italian hydraulic engineers. The leat is drawn off from a point above a fine flight of terraces, and is still in working order today.

Abinger Mill site dates back to the end of the eleventh century and was utilised for various industrial purposes throughout its history including gunpowder, copper utensils, and flour. Thomas Evershed was the tenant from 1845 to 1874 when Arthur Crane took over until it finally closed just before this picture was taken in 1890.

This picture of the pond was taken shortly after the closure. The mill was of ancient construction with three floors under a tiled roof seen just above the level of the water. It was demolished in the early years of this century and whilst the millpond has long since disappeared under a mass of vegetation, the attractive seventeenth-century millhouse has survived.

Crossways Farm was probably built around 1622 by a member of the Leigh family, and its frontage is a striking example of the vernacular style in brick. The building has a fine chimney stack and a substantial buttress which ties the house to the garden wall. The nearby barn is almost as old and the surrounding farmland occupies around 114 acres. The house is said to have been the inspiration for Meredith's novel *Diana of the Crossways*.

Raikes Lane crosses the stream just above Crossways Farm at a place known locally as Sleepy Hollow. In this photograph, taken around 1890, local photographer Walter Rose is emulating a similar pose used by the acclaimed victorian photographer, Col. Joseph Gale and also titled 'Sleepy Hollow'.

Paddington Mill takes its name from the fifeteenth-century farm which can be seen in the background. The pond was an extensive feature in the early years of this century when it was owned by the watercress firm R. & J. Coe. It was used by the local angling club until 1965 when it was filled in and now is just visible from the A25 as a depression in the fields.

The mill building itself is rather uninteresting and typical of the early Victorian period. This picture was taken after the pond had been drained but conveys the former picturesque surroundings. The watercress beds can be seen in the background.

The mill had a 10ft overshot water wheel which has long been removed for scrap, and above this the iron pentrough carries the inscription 'Thomas Spencer Millwright of Guildford', and in bolder letters 'W.J. Evelyn 1867'. At the time of writing the mill building is being restored prior to conversion to a three-storey dwelling.

# *Three*

# The Glade in the Hills

The Green, Holmbury St Mary.

12.

Holmbury St Mary is a comparatively new residential development born out of the coming of the railway to nearby Gomshall. Prior to the 1870s it comprised the two separate hamlets of Pitland Street and Felday, joined by an area known as the Glade which is now largely developed. The village centres on the Green, the church, and the Royal Oak public house – sadly the village shop has now closed.

In 1910 sheep were a common sight in Pitland Street. The sandy hills around the Hurtwood and Leith Hill remained dry in the winter and sheep from Romney Marsh in Kent would spend the winter here. Arriving by train at Gomshall they would be driven into the hills and back to Kent again in the spring.

The Kings Head public house is one of the oldest dwellings in Holmbury, built certainly before 1839. At the rear was once a brewhouse, and the picture shows the publican Mr Hutchins with his wife in the white apron standing among a group of local worthies.

Pub. by H. Bullen.

At the entrance to the village is post office corner, one of the highest points in the village. In a field to the right a spring rises to feed a small rill known as the Sutton Stream, which flows northwards to meet the Tillingbourne at Abinger. The turning to the left leads to the old post office.

In the thirties the post office was clearly offering more than just stamps. Locals and travellers alike were able to buy teas, cakes, ice cream, and cigarettes.

From 1895, and for most of this century, the Pitland Street post office has been run by the Bullen family. The picture possibly shows Harry Bullen on the right and his cousin Albert on the left. Godfrey Bullen was sub-postmaster up until the office closed.

Overlooking the Green is St Mary's Church, designed by the celebrated architect G.E. Street. Built in 1879, it is considered to be one of the best examples of the Decorated Gothic style in Surrey.

The Royal Oak overlooks the Green and was once the regular meeting place for the local fox hounds.

Much of the present village of Holmbury St Mary lies in the area known as the Glade. The neat houses and cottages nestle amongst the pines in a way that is reminiscent of Switzerland.

Many houses in the area are fine examples of the comparatively modern Surrey Village style. The red brick walls, hanging titles, and painted woodwork bear tribute to the Victorian appreciation of scale and location.

Raikes Farm at Sutton Abinger stands at the top of the lane behind the Volunteer public house. It was known at one time as Stone Age farm because of the many flint implements to be found in the fields in the neighbourhood.

On the lane leading down towards Abinger the road narrows suddenly at the hamlet of Sutton Abinger. The two seventeenth-century cottages retain much of their old world charm and the building beyond once housed the forge. A road branches to the right, and crosses the stream towards The Volunteer public house. At one time a dip-hole in front of the inn was the only source of water for Sutton's inhabitants.

# Four

# The Hammer in the Valley

Someone visiting Abinger Hammer for the first time might be excused for assuming that the name derived from the implement used by the blacksmith to strike the hours on the bell below the village clock. However its derivation dates back to much earlier times when the valley rang to the resounding clang of the trip hammer shaping raw pig iron into objects for homes, farms, and industry.

The firm of W. & G. King was established in Abinger in 1836 when William King started as a wheelwright, and took his nephew George as a partner. This picture, taken outside the old forge in 1870, shows some of the craftsmen with the various tools of their trades.

ESTABLISHED 1835.

W. & G. KING

Builders,

WHEELWRIGHTS & UNDERTAKERS,

SHOEING & GENERAL SMITHS,

*Abinger Hammer*

DORKING, SURREY.

ALL KINDS OF WOOD AND IRON FENCING.

*AGRICULTURAL IMPLEMENTS OF ALL KINDS MADE AND REPAIRED.*

ORDERS PUNCTUALLY ATTENDED TO.

This old label from the last century shows the extent of activities undertaken by the firm of Kings from their base in Abinger. As well as building and repairing wagons and agricultural implements they became one of the largest construction firms in the neighbourhood, and established brickyards at White Down and Holmbury.

The site now occupied by Martin Grant homes was taken over in the last century by Kings as a storage area for timber and building materials. For centuries before this it was the home of the giant trip hammer forge established by Thomas Elrington in the 1550s. The hammer pond was said to cover three acres in the area of the present watercress beds, and the mill continued until around 1787, when the industry moved north to be close to newly found coal.

King's yard would have provided ample opportunity for adventure and mischief making by the local children.

Abinger post office is shown here in 1910 at its original site next to W. & G. King's forge and general smithy. The timber clad building known as Grasmere was built around 1870 and has now reverted to being a private residence.

The proximity of the stream to the main road and the houses beyond can clearly be seen. The building to the left which is the present shop and post office was built for William King in 1881 and used as offices. Behind is Kings House, built around the same time for the other senior partner, Mr George King.

Abinger Hammer.    W.H.A.1258.

Once again the bourne moves calmly on its way through the village and past the village green, where cricket has been played since 1960. The ground was donated to the villagers by the owners of Abinger Hall as a memorial to those villagers who died in two World Wars.

Abinger's best known monument is the famous Hammer Clock. The present building occupies the site of the old blacksmith's shop and the original clock was constructed in 1891 as a memorial to T.H. Farrer of Abinger Hall. The clock was later removed to the stables of the Hall where it remains.

The new clock has existed in its present form since 1909. Carved in teak, it serves as a reminder of the long tradition of iron working in the village. The inscription reads 'By me you know how fast you go. For you at home I part the day 'twixt sleep and meals 'twixt work and play'.

Abinger Hall.

The old mansion by Sir John Scarlett was demolished by Thomas Farrer and Abinger Hall was rebuilt in a grand Victorian style in 1872. During his occupancy several bore holes were dug and a water wheel was installed in the bourne to pump water to a reservoir above the hall to feed fountains and other projects. The house was pulled down in 1959 and now only the gates, stable yard, and walled garden remain.

The Abinger Arms in 1890 before it was rebuilt. The timber-framed parts and the massive chimney date from the sixteenth century when it was a large house known as Perrotts standing in ten acres of land. William Rich was the innkeeper at the time.

In 1894 the building was enlarged and a new frontage and entrance added on the eastern side. The proprietor in 1902 was C. Rich, who later moved on to run the Stephan Langton at Friday Street.

46

William Rich was publican of the Abinger Arms from 1869 to 1900. He was clearly a great village character who enjoyed his pint out of his own individually styled mug. The inscription on the photograph informs us that public houses remained open from 6 a.m. - 10 p.m., and the cost of beer at the time was a penny a pint.

Coe Brothers, Watercress Growers, Abinger Hammer, Dorking.

As the old mill ponds fell into disuse watercress growing became a thriving industry in the area. The sandy valley floor and the abundance of spring water provide ideal growing conditions to this day. William Smith made the first beds below Paddington Mill, and the brothers Richard and John Coe succeeded him shortly afterwards.

The Coe's business was the first large scale watercress enterprise in England and employed up to thirty pickers and many more casual workers as packers.

The coming of the railway in 1849 opened up markets in London as well as northern cities such as Manchester and Liverpool. This wagon made regular trips to Gomshall station in time for the London train. The business went from strength to strength, and at one time an estimated twenty five acres were turned over to watercress growing in beds extending as far as Gomshall and Chilworth.

Watercress was packed into large flat baskets for despatch. These were supplied locally by, amongst others, a Mr Cobbett of the Basket Works, High Street, Guildford. This postcard is post marked in 1908 and the inscription on the back reads 'we regret we are unable to take any more flats just now', Coe Bros.

Hatch Farm is a splendid Tudor farmhouse built on the site of an older manor house, known as Harms Hatch. Situated on the outskirts of the village, it is actually in Shere parish and the name hatch indicates the existence of a gate across the road at the parish boundary.

# Five

# A Tannery
# in the Garden

This view of Gomshall illustrates clearly the central role played by the Tillingbourne in the life of the village at the end of the last century. Water is available for the watering of animals and the soaking of cartwheels. In contrast the tannery chimney reminds us of the importance of industry right in the heart of the community.

In Victorian times a large area of marshland to the south of the road stretched from the outskirts to almost the centre of the village. At the turn of the century drainage was improved and the area developed for the growing of watercress.

Another aspect of the marsh with Wonham Way and the railway embankment in the background.

The shop opposite station approach has served several purposes during its lifetime, and at one time was the village post office. When this picture was taken it was owned by the local Co-operative Society.

The post office is shown here soon after it moved to its present site. Amongst other things Messrs V. Jelley were purveyors of photographic picture postcards, many of which have been used to illustrate this section of the book.

The railway was opened in 1846 as part of the cross-country route between Reading and Tonbridge. At that time the location of the station was decided by the greatest number of people waiting at a given spot on a given day. A local story relates how the landlord of the Black Horse provided free beer for those willing to stand near the pub to ensure that the station was sited at Gomshall.

Between the wars the station was the centre for transportation and was instrumental in the growth of outlying areas like Holmbury. Materials for leather tanning, feed for farm animals, watercress from Abinger were just a few of the products that passed through the busy station. Sadly the buildings and sidings have gone and the site has a quiet, almost ghostly, air.

February 1904 was the occasion of a serious rail crash at Gomshall station. A soldiers special train conveying 150 men of the 2nd Northumberland Fusiliers ran off the rails causing serious injury to the driver, fireman, and three soldiers. After a pull up from Dorking, the line makes a steep descent and the speed seems to have more than the heavenly laden train could cope with.

The level crossing in Burrows Lane was manually operated in 1909. Now the keeper's cottage has gone and the gates have been replaced by an automatic barrier.

The Black Horse first appears in the rent rolls as a public house in 1823, although records of a malthouse and a brewery date back as far as 1690. More recently it has been converted into a fish restaurant.

This old photograph from the middle of the last century shows a very ambitious water landscape opposite the Black Horse. Presumably the patrons were able to enjoy their refreshment whilst admiring the splendour of the fountains.

There was a watermill in Gomshall when the Domesday record was compiled in 1086, and it was probably situated on the present site. In the seventeenth century expansion was necessary and the present brick and timber-framed construction dates from that time.

When the mill was converted to an overshot design, in 1839, the Bourne was damned and the embankments of the pond raised in relation to some of the adjoining buildings.

GOMSHALL MILL.       1150 Lloyd, Albury.

Gomshall Mill actually spans the Bourne and at one time comprised two twin overshot wheels, driving horizontal lay shafts which allows for an unusually low construction. In 1951 it was described by John Hillier, the well known authority on water mills, as a working mill. It closed in 1953 and remained derelict until 1964 when it was purchased by the present owners.

The post office has occupied several sites in the village and earlier this century it was situated in the bay of the mill nearest the road. At this time ownership of the mill had reverted to the Bray family and the tenants were the nephews of George Egerton. This area is currently used as the antique and gift shop.

58

GOMSHALL. 1194 LLOYD, ALBURY.

Looking from the packhorse bridge which leads to Goose Green, the course of the bourne is instantly recognisable today.

The Compasses was built around 1830 and originally was a beer shop. It became an inn in 1886 and was leased to the Guildford brewers Lascelles & Tickner when this picture was taken.

Gomshall.

W.H.A.
Photo Series 1255

Edmonds Farm is one of the oldest buildings in Gomshall, the earliest part dating from around 1450. Many additions have been made over the centuries and the chimney probably dates from around 1600. In the nineteenth century the Burchett family were the tenants of the house and the 150-acre farm and the present form of the building dates from 1830, including the stuccoed exterior and the monkey puzzle tree.

Gomshall village in the early 1900s is still recognisable today. The store in the foreground later became the tannery shop.

There has been a tannery in Gomshall since the sixteenth century and three were recorded in the eighteenth century. Some of the old buildings remain but most were rebuilt after a disastrous fire in 1892. The Evershed family are seen here in 1868. John Evershed and daughter Elsie are on the bridge and his wife Sophia and children Madge and John jnr. are in the foreground.

The tanyard in the nineteenth century was a hive of industry. The cart is filled with oak bark which was used in the tanning process. Leather tanning ceased in 1988 and the tannery shop continued selling leather goods from other sources until quite recently.

Most of the hides used were from local sources. Hair is removed using slaked lime prior to the tanning which uses tannic acid from oak bark.

Leather can be used in a variety of ways, depending on the method of treatment. Originally the main outlet for tannery products was in heavy harness, straps and saddlery. From 1930 the tannery was owned by the Union International Company and products tended towards softer clothing applications.

For most of the last century the tannery was owned by the Evershed family who can trace their presence in Surrey back to about 1200. In 1868 the family lived in the large house known as Jordells which, having passed through a series of conversions, is now the terrace of the houses numbered 2-9 Station Road.

These two delightful views show the extent to which the owners of the tannery house have taken full advantage of the Tillingbourne as a central feature of this idyllic landscape. The old packhorse bridge, dating from the sixteenth century, linked the house with the works and remains to this day.

Members of the Evershed family enjoying their surroundings. The small boy in the foreground was John who lived here until he was eight, when the family moved to Shalford. He spent much of his adult life in India but yearned to return to the Surrey Hills, finally purchasing High Brooms, Pitch Hill, near Ewhurst.

The Stream, Gomshall.

At Queen Street the Bourne turns sharply before continuing on its way towards Shere.

The large house on the left was formerly the Old Tannery and later known as Ivy House. The main part of the building is a fine brick Jacobean house built around 1620.

# Six

# The Prettiest
# in England

The Tillingbourne flows through the centre of Shere, a village which includes several houses of historic interest. This particular combination has led observers to dub the village 'the prettiest in England'. This view, which is part of the Surrey Photographic Survey taken in 1890, is largely obscured today due to the trees and undergrowth.

Netley Mill is recorded as far back as 1233 as belonging to the Abbey of Netley and was still in operation in the nineteenth century when the miller was one William King.

The Old Mill, Shere.

In 1931 the Hurtwood Water Company was formed to supply water to the area and Netley Mill was used to house the pump. When a new pumping station was opened, in 1952, the old mill was sold. The old mill pond which had become completely silted up has been reclaimed and now forms part of a carefully landscaped garden.

Just upstream from High House Farm is the site of the second of the two mills mentioned in Domesday. The buildings have long since been demolished but the restored pond and the weir can still be seen behind the Doctor's Surgery. This picture from the last century shows the pond being used for more pleasurable purposes.

SHERE.

LLOYD, ALBURY.

The stream flows on past High House Farm. The bridge carries the footpath from the church to the village school. On its way it passes the open-air swimming pool, one of the oldest still remaining today.

The Farm, Shere.

Watercress once grew in abundance along the banks of the Bourne and provided a valuable supplementary crop for the farm workers.

High House was the principal house in the manor of Shere Eborum and was recorded as a capital mansion in 1577 when it was sold by Lady Jane Bray to William Risbridger. This earlier house was pulled down and the present one was built around 1630. It is built in English bond with a queen strut roof of two storeys and attics with two rooms on each floor and a central chimney. William Bray bought back the manor and farm in 1771 and the name High House seems to date from this time.

In 1933 a group of undergraduates formed an acting group known as the 'Otherwise Club' and put on performances between July and August in an old hay barn owned by Mr Reginald Bray. Among the performers was a young Peter Ustinov who made his debut at seventeen. The eight performances a week were much enjoyed by the villagers until the wartime blackout forced closure and the building was commandeered by the army for the storage of armaments.

Middle Street boasts several houses of note. Bodryn, on the right, was built before 1500 and the jettied front added around 1600. It was originally the manorial court house but at the end of the last century it was in the ownership of Baverstocks, the local smithy who ran the adjacent forge. Beyond is the timber-framed tea shop designed by Edwyn Lutyens, and between this and the stream is the old fire station erected in 1885.

This unusual picture shows soldiers visiting the village in the First World War, much to the interest of the local children. The reason for the visit is unknown but possibly it was part of a recruiting campaign.

SHERE.

Middle Street in 1902 shows how the Bourne and the bridge are the centre of village life. A donkey cart provides a convenient form of transport and the horse enjoys a paddle.

The church overlooking the village in 1902. The house on the left, known as Pantrys, was once owned by William Southon, the owner of Gomshall Mill in the nineteenth century. Vaughans on the right was once the post office and the adjoining building included a blacksmiths shop.

The present church, dedicated to St James, dates from around 1190 and is built in a style known as Transitional. In the fourteenth century the anchoress Christine Carpenter was enclosed in a small cell at her own behest. The quatrefoil and squint through which she made her contacts with the church can still be seen.

The fine old elm trees dominated the square for many years and were a favourite play area for the village children. The shop on the corner was owned by Jay's the butchers when this picture was taken around 1910.

By the 1920s the motor car began to appear on the scene and Shere was within easy travelling distance from London. The White Horse was a favourite watering place but the tranquil agricultural economy was set to disappear.

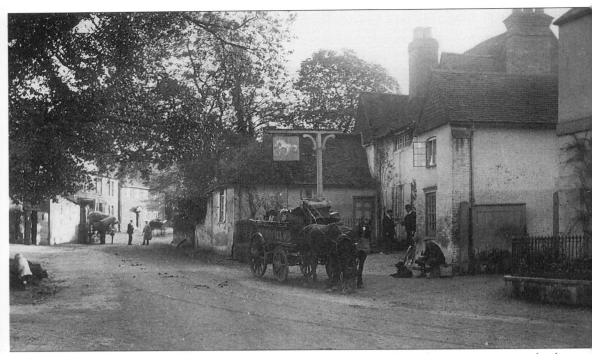

The White Horse was originally a dwelling but appears to have been an inn since the late seventeenth century when a brewhouse and later a hop garden were added at the back. The original innkeepers were the Morgan Sherlocks who kept house from around 1650-1730. The Askews managed the White Horse from 1866 to 1945 and during this time considerable alterations were made, including the new timbered frontage.

Prince of Wales, Shere.   Proprietor, J. Saunders.   Luncheons & Teas.

The Prince of Wales was also built as a private house but later than the White Horse. This advertising card shows the proprietor, Mr J. Saunders and his wife offering luncheons and teas.

The Coronation of George V in 1910 was an occasion of great celebration in the village. This Triumphal Arch was designed by Dr Cory, the village doctor at the time, and built by his newly formed troop of boy scouts.

After the bridge the bourne flows alongside Lower Street and the grassy bank remains an attraction for visitors even to this day. The house on the right is known as Lavender House, a reminder of the days when locally grown lavender products were sold in the shop, then called Lavender Ladye.

Further along Lower Street, past the Old Prison and the Old Forge, the road swings to the right to join Rectory Lane. An old wooden bridge is provided for the convenience of pedestrians whilst the narrow ford is one of the few still remaining in the county.

THE RECTORY FROM LIME WALK. SHERE

Beyond the ford is the tree-lined avenue known as Lime Walk. From here can be gained the odd glimpse of the Old Rectory built in 1844 and enlarged in 1859. It replaced an earlier timber-framed parsonage which stood nearer the Tillingbourne and had been the home of the Duncumbs, who were rectors of Shere between 1658 and 1843.

At the end of Lime Walk is the Rectory Bridge which at one time served as an entrance to the rectory. The ornate wooden balustrade has subsequently been replaced by a more functional brick built structure.

Shallow waterfalls are to be found along the length of the Tillingbourne, such as the one between Shere and the bounds of Albury Park.

This rather ornate mock-Tudor chalet was built, probably as an estate worker's cottage, in the last century. Chantry Lane forms the boundary between Shere and Albury and the chalet lies just in the latter parish.

# Seven

# The Village that Moved

Much of the present village of Albury lies in what was formerly the hamlet of Weston Street. The site of the original village lies a mile to the east in Albury Park. The river runs to the north of the village but later crosses under the road before disappearing between brick arches into the fields.

SILENT-POOL, **ALBURY.**

Many legends surround the origins and history of the Silent Pool, most of which can be attributed to the creative pen of Martin Tupper. There are in fact two ponds – the upper and lower, and in former times a thatched arbour was provided to allow the visitor to enjoy the tranquillity of the surroundings.

LOWER-POOL, **ALBURY.**

The Sherbourne spring provides a constant source of clear water and was dug to provide a supply to the decorative gardens of Albury Park. Home Farm on the other side of the A25 has much machinery which was designed to be driven by water supplied from the Silent Pool.

THE COTTAGE, SILENT-POOL.

Earlier this century the Silent Pool became a popular spot for trippers making a detour from Newlands Corner or Boxhill. The bicycle was clearly a popular form of transport when this picture was taken in 1902.

Silent Pool Cottage, Albury.

S.W. Series. 1110.

Around the time of the First World War, the motor car became the smart mode of transport and the old cottage was replaced by a more modern building with a tea garden to cater for this new found trade.

The mansion has changed hands many times over the centuries but owes much of its present appearance to Henry Drummond, who purchased it in 1819. He was responsible for many alterations to the house and gardens including the chimneys, said to be designed, or at least influenced by, Augustus Pugin.

The park extends to some 150 acres and contains many rare trees although the storms of 1987 and 1990 caused much devastation. The gardens were laid out by John Evelyn in the seventeenth century and incorporate some of the features from the gardens at Wotton, especially the extensive use of water.

The Bourne flows on through the park past the site of the old village, now largely removed as a result of nineteenth-century landscaping. Records show the presence of an ancient corn mill which was destroyed by fire in 1727 following an explosion of the gunpowder stored there. It was rebuilt and later converted to a paper mill before it finally disappeared in the last century.

Henry Drummond became an ardent supporter of Edward Irving and paid for the building of the Apostolic church in 1840. The second coming of the Lord was central to their belief and the church was administered by twelve Apostles who were designated by Divine guidance. The church is seldom used but is still maintained, in anticipation of a second Advent.

Old Parish Church, Albury Park.

The 'old church' is all that remains of the original village which disappeared, bit by bit, after 1780. The building, some of which dates from Saxon times, was allowed to decay until 1921 when it was restored by the Churches Conservation Trust and the new chancel added. Services are still held here at Midsummer and Christmas.

The entrance to Albury village is not immediately recognisable today. The field on the left is now a trout fishery and is largely obscured by undergrowth.

At the entrance to The Street is the large walled garden of Weston House which in recent times was owned by the well known naturalist and author, Dr Maurice Burton. There are records of an earlier rather grand Palladian mansion standing on the site but, when this was gutted by fire, Henry Drummond made sure it was demolished as he did not wish to have such an imposing house nearby to rival his own Albury Park Mansion.

Weston yard was for many centuries the farmyard of the Manor of Weston. The old Tudor pigeon house is remarkable for being octagonal and built of brick. It once housed up to 600 birds which provided meat in winter and their droppings were used for fertiliser and in the manufacture of gunpowder in the local mills.

S. & W. Series

THE POST OFFICE, ALBURY

Next to the old hall and the schoolmasters house is a large building divided into three and noted for its 'Pugin' chimneys so characteristic of the Albury skyline. The house at the east end is intriguingly dubbed 'Not the Old Pharmacy'. The central portion is Farrier's cottage and the post office was located in the section nearest the camera.

The present Drummond Arms replaced an older hostelry known as the Running Horse. At the turn of the century beer was supplied by the local Albury Brewery, which is actually housed in the left hand portion of the building.

The gardens at the rear of the Drummond Arms slope gently down to the banks of the stream where trout can be seen and numerous ducks and other waterfowl add a natural feature to these idyllic surroundings.

Martin Tupper, the prolific Victorian author and poet, lived in Albury House during the middle of the nineteenth century. The story of Stephen Langton and the Silent Pool did much to create interest in the local history of the area, and at one time Tupper was expected to be appointed Poet Laureate. His burial vault can be seen in the graveyard of the old Saxon church.

Children from Albury Village School in 1921 taking part in a concert put on for the benefit of parents and local residents. Some of those taking part are still living in the area.

Weston Lea stands on the corner of Church Lane and The Street. When this picture was taken in 1868 the property was owned by Henry Drummond and occupied by John Evershed and his family who farmed the land on the estate. Later it was occupied by Mr T. Botting of Albury Mill and in 1878 the appearance of the house changed considerably when it was enlarged by the then owner, the 6th Duke of Northumberland.

Albury's village green must be the smallest in the country and there is little room for more than the signpost standing in the centre. The present structure was restored by the Albury Trust in 1983 but the original model, seen here, was surmounted by a lantern, lit every evening by the lamplighter. Pratts Stores continues to provide the village supplies and now houses the post office.

The Tillingbourne has long been the life-blood of the village and the flow remains largely constant even in times of drought. The bridge provides a crossing for through traffic whilst still allowing access for horses and cartwheels.

The charming old cottage on the corner of Church Lane and Blackheath Lane dates from the sixteenth century. The timber-framed construction remains largely unchanged with the possible exception of the wooden gutters and down pipes which have subsequently been replaced by cast iron models.

The parish church of St Peter and St Paul stands high above the village and is inspired by designs encountered by Henry Drummond on his trips to France. The brick construction is rather austere and the church was consecrated in 1842. The pleasant interior owes much to the generosity of the Duke of Northumberland and his wife Louisa – the daughter of Henry Drummond.

Birmingham Lane, Albury (42)

The lane leading past Birmingham Farm is typical of so many north/south tracts which traverse this region. The combined forces of nature and the hand of man have merged to carve a deep ravine no more marked in Surrey than here in Albury.

Waterloo Ponds.    Albury.

On the outskirts of Albury is the house known as Vale End overlooking Waterloo Ponds. The main road is new and a small track leading off to the right is the old road to Guildford which can be seen on the right of this picture. At the western end of the pond it is still possible to see the wheel pit, all that remains of an old paper mill known as Postford Upper mill which closed in the 1830s.

"Surrey Hills" Holiday Resort, Albury.

Further along the new road is the entrance to Surrey Hills, now the premises of the local village club, but between the wars the property was described as a 'holiday resort'.

The Surrey Hills overlooks lower Postford Pond. Pictures from the turn of the century recall this splendid looking timber-framed house which sadly has since been destroyed.

Post Ford Ponds, Albury.  S&W Series. 58

Postford lower mill is on the site of a former paper mill which later became a flock mill until it finally closed in the 1890s. When Botting's Mill in the village was destroyed by arson in 1909 the business moved to the larger site at Postford.

## Eight

# The Rill
# from the Hill

*Coverwood Old Farm House, Peaslake.*

Lawbrook, a second tributary of the Bourne, arises in springs which form into a series of naturalised lakes in the area known as Coverwood Farm. The gardens, originally comprising some twenty-four acres, were laid out around 1910 when Mr Stephens of Stephen's Ink fame purchased the land and built Coverwood House. The natural springs feed a bog garden which, although ravaged by recent storms, contains many specimen trees which are enjoyed by hundreds of visitors.

The rill from Coverwood flows northwards, emerging from the fields to run alongside Ewhurst Road. At one time the area was known as Peaslick Bottom. The spire of St Mark's church can been seen on the left.

Along the Ewhurst Road some splendid old houses can been seen including Western cottages which was formerly the workhouse. The furthest of the pair of cottages on the right was once the village dairy.

The little bridge at the centre of the village is a feature of many old photographs, but earlier this century the ditch was culverted to enable the road to be widened. The old off-licence and cottages on the right were demolished in the 1920s to make way for the Hurtwood Inn.

Peaslake Village. Up until the first part of the last century the brook ran through the centre of the village. The building on the left was the butcher's shop.

Brook is a small community which seems to have grown up around the impressive seventeeth-century Brook Manor. This charming picture of the simple life earlier this century shows the steam engine in use on the farm whilst the horse takes a welcome drink from the pond.

Here the local children pose for their picture in the farm wagon in front of Brook cottage. The detached cottages are known today simply as Northside and Southside cottages and the building on the right was once the village post office and stores.

The Lawbrook runs through its own little valley towards Little Ford Farm. The area was once developed by Coes as part of their watercress empire but today the ponds are still put to good use as a trout farm.

*Nine*

# Damnable Inventions

The church of St Martha on the Hill has stood on its present site overlooking the valley for a thousand years. Nothing remains of an earlier Saxon church but the present building dates from around 1087. St Martha's stands between two ancient tracks, the Ridgeway in the north and the so called Pilgrim's Way in the south. After falling into disrepair, restoration was completed in the middle of the last century so that modern day pilgrims are still able to enjoy its tranquil charm.

THE SCHOOLS, CHILWORTH.

When the old village school opened in 1873 it claimed to be the first to offer free education in the country. At one time it catered for sixty pupils but as the number of young children grew it became apparent that a bigger school was needed. When the new school opened in 1967 the old building was demolished as part of a scheme to widen the road to Dorking.

St. Martha's Chapel, from Chilworth.

On entering Chilworth from the west the A248 crosses one of the ancient tracks known as Lockner Road. The entrance to Lockner Farm is on the right and the old square barn remains to the present day. This track leads down to a bridge over the stream to the site of the old gunpowder mills, the remains of which are still visible.

The house now known as Aston Villas was originally a grocer's shop owned by A. Shepard. By 1927 ownership had transferred to A.A. Lemon and the road signs attest to the ascendancy of the motor car.

The Percy Arms was named after the Percy family and dates back to the 1880s. It was once the centre of village life and also offered bed and breakfast. The frontage was originally closer to the road and the building underwent considerable alteration in 1969.

In earlier times a room on the ground floor was pressed into service as a mortuary for the unfortunate victims of explosions at the gunpowder works.

Chilworth Station.

The railway arrived in 1849 and was powered by steam locomotives until diesel took over in 1965. In earlier times there would have been much goods traffic in the form of livestock, flour from Bottings Mill, coal from merchants Shepard & Hayward, and of course gunpowder from the mills. The station buildings remain and the 127-year-old footbridge which used to span the platform was about to be broken up but was saved by local artist David Shepherd and moved to the East Somerset Railway in 1978.

Built to provide accommodation for the railway workers, Railway Cottages were owned by the South Eastern Railway. In 1888 agreement was reached to link the tramway from the gunpowder works with the railway so that gunpowder could be transported by train. The building at the end used to be the post office, managed by Mr and Mrs Field.

The coming of the railway in 1849 necessitated a change in the layout of the road to Godalming. Tangley crossing was installed and 'New Road' laid out which made way for the present development of houses, bungalows, and shops.

Chilworth Village.

Blacksmith's Lane provides a bridge over the stream and the remains of the millrace from an ancient corn mill. The old paper mill buildings were along the left of the lane and the lodge entrance to the old gunpowder mills can be seen on the right.

Chilworth Cottage.

Further up the lane stands this old cottage which now forms an integral part of Halfpenny Corner. In Victorian times it would have overlooked the paper mills and later Unwins printing works until they were destroyed in a disastrous fire in 1895.

The mill dam was probably the site of the corn mill listed in the Domesday survey of 1086. The dam has been raised over the centuries and the 14 foot head of water would have been sufficient to drive at least two overshot wheels. Fulling mills and wire mills were recorded before this area became the lower gunpowder works. Recently this view has become largely obscured by undergrowth but listening to the tumbling water remains a moving experience.

With waterways being the arteries of the gunpowder works, boats provided a convenient and safe means of transport. This rare photograph shows Bert Hammond and a workmate in 1913 working the punts on the millstream conveying the partially completed powder to the next stage of the process. The powder is packed into barrels with specially made leather covers.

Nellie Hamley (née Peters) in the uniform of the Chilworth gunpowder factory in the First World War. When labour became short women were drafted in to carry on essential tasks previously an exclusively male province.

Some remaining features of the old Admiralty works can still be seen from the footpath. The pond was created in 1983 and the substantial building beyond was once a stove used in the manufacture of cordite.

This row of cottages was converted from a former cordite press house by the Duke of Northumberland before he sold the site in 1922. In the 1980s they had become rather run down and were rebuilt in a more modern style, although the old dividing walls appear to have been retained.

The Tillingbourne ... Guildford.

After its exertions through Chilworth, the Bourne once again returns to its tranquil meandering course through the meadows. The railway line can be seen on the left and the whole picture is overseen by St Martha on the hill.

# Ten

# A Shallow Ford

SHALFORD.

Shalford or 'shallow ford' was the village where the Tillingbourne had to be crossed by traffic travelling south from Guildford in ancient times. The bridge was completed in 1758, shortly after the opening of the turnpike road to Newbridge through Alfold and Loxwood. The prosperity of Shalford was later enhanced by the arrival of the canal in 1816 and the railway in 1849.

Tillingbourne Stream & Old Cottages, East Shalford.    S&W. Series. 584.

Until the middle of the nineteenth century East Shalford was situated on the main route between Godalming and the industries of Chilworth and Gomshall. The advent of the railway changed that as the line required the opening of a new road and the installation of a level crossing.

Old Cottage, East Shalford.    S&W Series. 575.

The comparative isolation of the eastern end of Shalford has left a small community of quaint old cottages which relish their tranquillity and proximity to the stream.

Shalford Mill in the 1890s before its conversion to a dwelling and the addition of windows on the eastern elevation. A mill was recorded on this site in the Domesday Book and the present building dates from the eighteenth century. It originally belonged to the Godwen-Austen family and was a working corn mill until 1914 when it was allowed to fall into a dilapidated state. In 1932 it was rescued by a dedicated band of preservationists known as the Ferguson's Gang and presented to the National Trust.

Near the junction between East Shalford Lane and The Street, the stream passes under the lane once again. There would have been a ford here in earlier times and, when bridged, the stream was left available to provide water for passing horses.

The Street in 1900 gives an indication of the effects of horse drawn traffic in this narrow road which was often given to flooding. The cottage facing down the lane was once a post office and sweet shop until it was joined with the adjacent building to become the Toco Chintz Tea Shoppe. It was bought by Mr Samuel Lofting in 1922 and remained a tea shop until 1960 and confectionery was still sold up until 1987.

Close to the church stood the entrance to Shalford House, seat of the Godwen-Austen family from 1600 until it was sold in 1899. It remained in private hands for another decade until it was converted into a private hotel which it remained until 1935.

Shalford House was an impressive building standing in acres of parkland. It passed through a series of private ownerships but was allowed to run down to such an extent that the borough council authorised its demolition to make way for the Thames Water abstraction scheme completed in 1976.

Among the amenities enjoyed by the hotel residents was a nine-hole golf course amid the splendid parkland surroundings. This area between the River Wey and the A281 has now been cleared and levelled to make way for a playing field.

Shalford Park from St. Catherines. 86. S.&W. Series.

Seen from St Catherine's, the house could be appreciated in its natural splendour across the wide bow of the River Wey. Although not visible in this view, the Tillingbourne joins the river at a point somewhere at the right of the picture.

The Old Toll House as it would have appeared to travellers and local farmers in around 1870.

Park cottages on the Shalford Road were once the original toll house on the turnpike south of Guildford. This picture, taken shortly after the great storm of 1905, shows a fallen tree which caused considerable damage to the property. The inscription on the postcard reads, 'the Bedroom to the right of the Fallen Trees is that in which a bedridden man, aged 78 was lying. He escaped unhurt.'

RIVER WEY, GUILDFORD.

Having joined the Wey, the combined river flows on past Shalford Meadows towards Guildford.
The river is navigable at this point and the old towing path can be seen on the left.

ST. CATHARINE'S FERRY, GUILDFORD.

LLOYD, GUILDFORD.

Earlier this century crossings of the river between St Catherine's and Shalford were made by
ferry in the form of punt. This is thought to be the route taken by pilgrims centuries before.

RIVER WEY, **GUILDFORD.**

Near to the stretch now used by the canoe club the river swings north once again near the Jolly Farmer public house. The old boat house seen here is no longer in existence although traces of it can still be found.

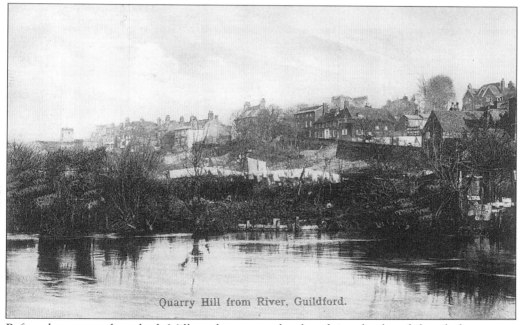

Quarry Hill from River, Guildford.

Before the new road was built Millmead was an undeveloped river bank and the whole area was liable to flooding. It is barely recognisable now but Quarry Street can be seen in the background.

127

# Bibliography

Alexander, Matthew: *Tales of Old Surrey*, Countryside Books, 1987.
Albury Trust: *A Short Guide to the Parish*, 1994.
Brandon, Dr Peter: *The Tillingbourne River Story*, 1984.
Cobbett, William: *Rural Rides*, Penguin Classics, 1985.
Corke, Shirley: *Abinger Hammer, A short history and guide*, 1993.
Crocker, Glenys: *A Guide to the Chilworth Gunpowder Mills*, 1990, and 1994.
Harding, Keith: *Dorking and District in Old Photographs*,
Alan Sutton Publishing, 1993.
Hawkins, Christopher: *Hidden Surrey*, 1987.
Morris, J.E.: *Black's Guide to Surrey*, 1920.
O'Kelly, Terence: *Abinger Common and Wotton*, 1988.
Parker, Eric: *Highways & Byways in Surrey*, 1908.
Shalford Parish Council: *Portrait of a Surrey Parish*, 1995.
Shere, Gomshall, and Peaslake Local History Society: *A Short History*, 1981.
The Parish of Shere: *Pictorial Record, Shere Parish Council*, 1993.
Shere, Gomshall, and Peaslake Local History Society:
*Old Houses in the Parish of Shere*, 1981.
Schupke, S.A.: *A History of Chilworth*, 1994.
Stidder, Derek: *The Watermills of Surrey*, Barracuda Books, 1990.
Warner, D.W.: *Chilworth Gunpowder Mills, Surrey History* Vol. 1, No. 4, 1976.